Over Under

Marthe Jocelyn • Tom Slaughter

Tundra Books

Published in Canada by Tundra Books,
75 Sherbourne Street, Toronto, Ontario M5A 2P9

Published in the United States by Tundra Books of Northern New York,
P.O. Box 1030, Plattsburgh, New York 12901

Library of Congress Control Number: 2004103919

National Library of Canada Cataloguing in Publication

Jocelyn, Marthe
    Over under / Marthe Jocelyn ; illustrated by Tom Slaughter.

ISBN 0-88776-708-7

    1. Space perception–Juvenile literature. 2. Size perception–Juvenile
literature. I. Slaughter, Tom II. Title.

BF469.J63 2005   j153.7'52   C2004-902033-1

We acknowledge the financial support of the Government of Canada through the
Book Publishing Industry Development Program (BPIDP) and that of the Government
of Ontario through the Ontario Media Development Corporation's Ontario Book Initiative.
We further acknowledge the support of the Canada Council for the Arts and the Ontario
Arts Council for our publishing program.

Design: Kong Njo
Medium: Painted paper cuts

ISBN-13: 978-0-88776-708-1
ISBN-10: 0-88776-708-7

Printed and bound in Hong Kong, China

2 3 4 5 6   10 08 07 06 05

For our mothers, Ginny and Joy

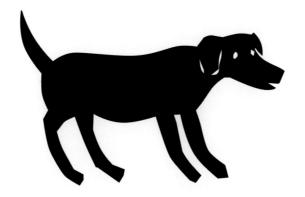

big

small

not at all

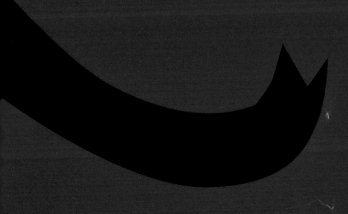

very short

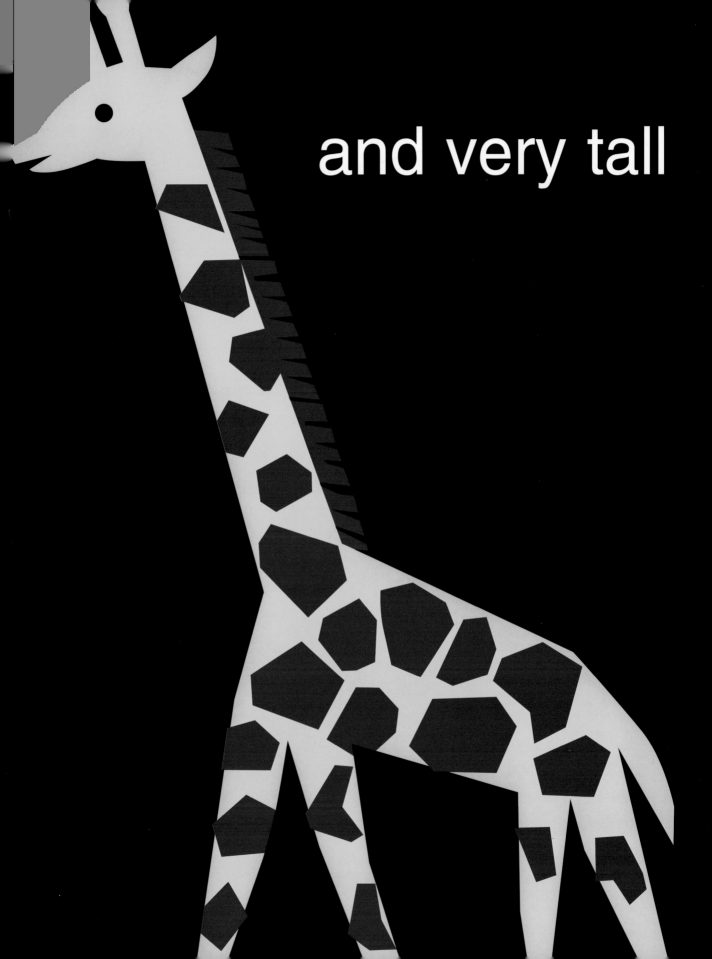

and very tall

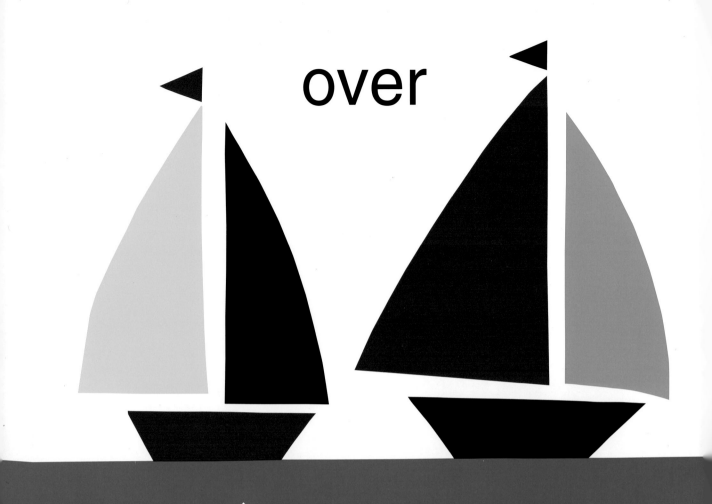

over

under

up

and
down

inside

outside

country

town

above is sky

below is ground

a square is square

a circle's round

sometimes black

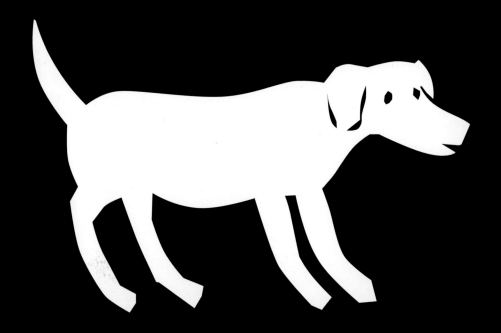

sometimes white

light is day

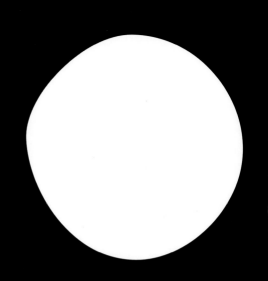

and dark
is night